Can Board Chairmen Get Measles?

Thirty years of great cartoons from
THE WALL STREET JOURNAL

Can Board Chairmen Get Measles?

edited by Charles Preston

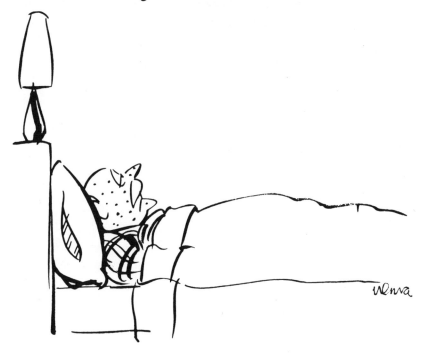

CROWN PUBLISHERS, INC.
NEW YORK

Copyright © 1982 by Cartoon Features Syndicate
All rights reserved. No part of this book may be reproduced
or transmitted in any form or by any means,
electronic or mechanical, including photocopying, recording,
or by any information storage and retrieval system,
without permission in writing from the publisher.
Published by Crown Publishers, Inc.,
One Park Avenue, New York, New York 10016
and published simultaneously in Canada
by General Publishing Company Limited
Manufactured in the United States of America
Library of Congress Cataloging in Publication Data
Main entry under title:
Can board chairmen get measles?
1. Business—Caricatures and cartoons.
2. Industry—Caricatures and cartoons. 3. American
wit and humor, Pictorial. I. Preston, Charles,
1921-   . II. Wall Street Journal.
NC1428.W33C3   1983   741.5′973   82-13079
ISBN: 0-517-54898-4
10 9 8 7 6 5 4 3 2 1
First Edition

Introduction

IF, AS A PRESIDENTIAL SAGE ONCE DECLARED, "THE business of America is business," I submit that much of the humor of America is to be found in the comedy of American business. For proof of that contention, you have only to look at *The Wall Street Journal*'s daily humor column, "Pepper...and Salt."

Every working day, for more than thirty years, the *Journal* cartoonists have observed and made comic comments about life on the funny side of The Street. The Street is where it all happens, where the merchants, managers, workers, and executives carry on the business of business, touching through their work the lives of virtually every person in America.

The cartoons on the following pages represent more than three decades of "Pepper...and Salt" flavoring. Earning and spending money need not be as grim as Karl Marx predicted; that is the substance of our Comic Manifesto.

CHARLES PRESTON

The 1950s

THE DECADE FOLLOWING WORLD WAR II FOUND THE nation in the euphoria of a bull market. Gasoline was 25¢ per gallon and the annual inflation rate—an endless source of complaint—was a killing 2 percent. Everyone was buying a piece of America. Bankers were heroes. Corporate mergers became a way of life. Much of what we found funny then, we still find funny, but some of yesterday's humor has now become the stuff of burning social issues. (I shudder at some of our sexist gags—which are included here for their historic value and, it is hoped, to show us how far we have come. . . .)

"Wilkins never wastes a minute, J.P.—that's his lunch."

"It could be just a coincidence, I suppose—but sometimes I wonder
if it's the government's way of rubbing it in."

"I have no friends...only contacts."

"Let me, Boss—it all goes on my expense account anyway."

"I wish *I* had the nerve to hire
a good-looking male secretary!"

"I was hoping you could suggest a highly speculative stock
that's never failed to pay a dividend."

"I *know* you're my wife. But I'm afraid we still require two pieces of identification."

"Up three points, please."

"All I ever get is checks!"

"I was a personnel manager."

"Remember son—money doesn't grow on trees;
it bubbles up from the ground."

14

"Do we get an employee discount?"

"Which analyst do you want? Stock, tax, or psycho?"

"Actually, I'm not in any tax bracket. Why?"

"There's apparently been a little misunderstanding about our merger."

"Will someone *else* please second the nomination?!"

"Of course I'll endorse that check.
What do you want me to say about it?"

"All right. Tell the butcher to hold his check until next Thursday;
ask the milkman not to cash his for two weeks and don't mail the one
to Lacy's Department Store until after the fifteenth!
Whew! It sure feels good to get them paid off!"

"All of it is being withheld and you owe us
an additional twelve dollars and twenty-two cents."

"You're the kind of man we need around here!"

"Hidden taxes were my downfall.
I hid mine fifteen years!"

"The way I figure it you have to *look* money to make money."

"Hmm! Geography up one and an eighth—spelling off
two and three quarters...."

"You're a banker? What a beautiful way to express one's self."

"I will *not*. *You* put *your* boss on first."

"As you know, gentlemen, business thrives on competition.
And to prove it, we have just bought out
another of our competitors."

"Can we have another tablecloth?"

"Frankly, Mr. Deegan, I find it hard to believe that
the entire New York Stock Exchange is out to get you."

"And furthermore, I distinctly remember dropping a check for you
in the mailbox at least a week ago. Therefore, gentlemen,
I can see no reason...."

"At these prices you should have been selling, not buying."

"All this financial chit-chat is Greek to little ol' me.
Do you intend to avoid the after-acquired clause through
creation of a subsidiary company or by consolidation?"

"I must say, for an industrial giant,
you're quite a disappointment."

The 1960s

BEADS AND BEARDS BECAME GRIST FOR THE COMIC mills of the '60s. Transcendental mantras were heard in brokers' offices and the Consumer Price Index became a fit subject for social protest. Conglomeration replaced invention as the new source of wealth. Did Dr. Spock's permissiveness precede the spectre of spiraling inflation that, to our horror, reached 3 percent a year? Billions still seemed like a lot but it wouldn't be that long until we'd be speaking of trillions. . . .

"Old Moneybags speaking."

"Every Monday it's the same thing. But you're still always
on that 8:13 bus!"

"How come *our* stocks never get into proxy fights?"

"He tosses billions around as though they were millions."

"I've got a job with a real challenge—getting there and back."

"But I'm not so sure I *want* a turned-on stock broker!"

"Will Consolidated Dynamics reach a new high for the year?
Can Mapac Electronics possibly recover the losses sustained in the
last hours of trading? And what about Raytexco—are the merger
rumors really true? Tune in again tomorrow...."

"We've discontinued the practice of sending bright young
junior executives to the university for specialized training."

"Can't you finish your MBA and then relate to humanity
on the side or something?"

"For heaven's sake, Walter. Can board chairmen get measles?"

"Give it to me straight, J.E., am I being eased out?"

"Charles is alone with his memories."

"My goodness, Howard—you make fiscal responsibility
sound like such *fun*!"

"What's on sale?"

"I suppose it was inevitable!"

"Gracious, I don't want to bring him back. I'd just like
his advice on some investments."

"Our record profits are eating up our valuable tax losses!"

"You mean for twenty-three years *your* work has consisted
of checking *my* work?"

"It's a regular contract with the standard loopholes."

"No, the bald one is the poet. The other one's
an investment counselor."

"Sorry, but a mantra isn't sufficient collateral."

"If you really want to protest something, why don't you sing
about the Consumer Price Index."

"Don't bother to get up—I'm just passing through."

"Okay, Harvey, get down to Brownell, Brownell, Durston, and Fisk and do your thing."

"What have you got for the man who is getting nowhere?"

"I said proxies, Miss Hamilton, not pixies."

"Well, most of my experience
has been posing for stock certificates."

"Mirror, mirror on the wall. Who is the new chairman of the board of the Tristate Folding Box Corporation?"

"Oh, yes, the check is signed—right there
between the setting sun and the lonesome pine."

"Happy Fiscal New Year!"

"I wish you could get it through your head, Grace, that millionaires
can no longer afford to *live* like millionaires."

The Early 1970s

AGAINST THE BACKDROP OF OUR WITHDRAWAL FROM Vietnam and the drama of Watergate, the '70s economy began a painful turn downward. Tight money, inflation that was not much of a joke, and a jarring oil crisis brought insecurity and, in its wake, the guru, into fashion. Conglomerators made room for consultants and semanticists as we tried to understand stagflation, money market funds, and the smug little silicon chip. Ecology became a buzzword. The bear market took over....

"...just for opening a new savings account for $2,500 or adding $2,500 to your existing account."

"If *you're* not making any money, and the *packer* isn't making any money, and the *rancher* isn't making any money, then the *cows* must have a helluva bundle stashed away."

"Here's a bit of nostalgia for you. I'm saving exactly the same amount per week *now* as I did when I was in grade school."

"You're sluggish—I'm sluggish. So why shouldn't
the economy be sluggish?"

"Believe me, the whole economy profits. We rob someone of five grand.
Then we buy some stuff from a fence. He gives his cut
to the mob. They pay off the cops...."

"And if your loan payment is in the mail,
please disregard these insults."

"I've got him softened up—now what is it we're selling?"

"Let's call a wildcat bankruptcy."

"I said sexist, Mr. Marsh. *Not* sexiest."

"Yes, Farber—you wished to speak to me?"

"Another successful year, gentlemen. We broke even on operations
and pulled a net profit on accounting procedures."

"Ms. Ryan, send me in a scapegoat."

"We've *got* a dummy corporation.
What we need is a smarty corporation."

"Let's see if I have this straight. You want a federal grant
to start a taxpayer's revolt?"

BURBANK

"It's Mrs. Hawthorne. She wants to know what sirloin
opened at today."

"Last week I'm running an electronics plant in Ohio—this week
I'm a holy man in Kashmir. You gotta admit I've got me one helluva
sharp tax lawyer!"

"I'm sorry, operator, that you accidentally refunded my money. No, I will not
re-deposit it, but if you'll leave your name and address,
I'll be happy to mail it to you."

"I bet you thought you'd never find a conservative
this far down the economic scale."

"Do you realize that this railroad is in worse financial shape than we are?"

"Do you have any qualifications other than good vibes?"

"I'm sorry, sir. You can't list a blown mind
as a capital loss."

"Are you sure you won't quit after a year
or two to get married?"

"Those were the days! Recruiters from G.M., G.E., 3M, Litton, Du Pont
swarming all over the place waving money!"

"Just sign on the dotted line and your industry will be deregulated."

"I tried everything—tax incentives, kickbacks, payoffs,
loopholes—and they all worked."

"What a *glorious* day for a proxy fight!"

"My father is an industrial polluter. What's yours?"

"It's very authentic, complete with stethoscope, blood pressure kit,
instruments, a diversified investment portfolio, trust fund,
and tax shelters."

"Which came first, the wage boost or the price hike?"

"I know how proud of it you are, Hodgekiss, but—"

"I didn't ask you where you got the money so why should you ask me
what I'm going to do with it?"

"We've reviewed your financial situation and decided
we don't want to get involved."

"If God hadn't wanted an oil depletion allowance, He wouldn't have created an oil lobby."

"I searched the whole world over. Then, one day,
I found happiness in my own backyard."

"Our sermon today is entitled 'The Meaning of God in a Bear Market.'"

"Cheap money or no cheap money, it's still something to be a billionaire."

"I can tell you this much—get out of transportations
and into industrials."

"Did you ever try to explain to your kid that you spend all day
buying and selling things that you don't have?"

Current Quandaries...

ON THE HEELS OF THE ACCOUNTANTS AND THEIR ledgerdemain, enter The Economists. Fancy new terms like supply-side, trickle-down, and disinflation are bandied about, but it seems that there's still no one who can explain how rising prices can possibly go side-by-side with unemployment. Even as the dollar declines and windfall profits soar, most of us agree that the system still works. Still, many elements in the system are changing; yesterday's timid secretary is becoming today's new executive and male chauvinists are finally getting their comeuppances.

As the computer comes of age and the sound of the Space Invaders is heard in the land, the *Journal* cartoonists will be on hand to record and offer comic comments to make it all bearable.

"Don't be ridiculous. You *can't* have inflation and recession
at the same time."

"I thought you'd be glad to know I hadn't lost faith in the dollar."

"When you say 'Your guess is as good as mine,' is that
a recommendation to buy, sell, or hold?"

"I now pronounce you a two-income household."

"If your wife thinks you're worth more money, Harper, perhaps you should go to work for her."

"My next tune makes a statement about our high-technology,
energy-consuming society."

"You won't have to worry about the high interest rates.
Your mortgage loan application has been turned down."

BANKRUPTCY
COURT

"This is a general tax alert! Everyone to the tax shelter!"

"We have to overcome your obsession with inflation...and by the way, my fee has gone up from $75 to $100 a session."

"I'm sorry, sir...but we can't honor your robbery request unless you have an account at this branch."

"No, I can't say I've profited from my own mistakes.
Mostly, I've profited from others' mistakes."

"Hey, man, you're really aces with us! We always figured you
white-collar crime cats would act uppity in here."

"I'm afraid complications have developed; his check bounced."

"There's a $20,000 bonus for anyone who can come up with
a euphemism for 'windfall profits.'"

"Do you have any other identification, sir?"

"I'll have the Businessman's Lunch and he'll have
the Lackey's Lunch."

"Look here, Caruthers! *I've* got to survive, *too*!"

"Five bucks! By god, the system does work!"

"We've done it again. We've disposed of all our disposable income."

"Here, I'm a rabid environmentalist.
At work, I'm a ruthless capitalist."

"We find that Folbert works better under pressure."

"No, I'm not a career girl. Are you a career boy?"

"I want a diversified portfolio providing growth potential
and a flexible tax base."

"There won't be any extras. $895.50 includes
everything I can think of."

"Let me assure you that to us, here at First National,
you're not just a number. You're two numbers, a dash,
three more numbers, another dash, and another number."

"Relax, kid, and just pitch to him as you would
to any other millionaire."

"I would like to order a pair of overalls and ten shares of AT&T."

"I took advantage of an offer where it was prohibited by law."

"Put your money in your mattress."

"I know 2 million's a lot of money, but you get
a $200 rebate check direct from the factory."

"You know, Charlie, it's hard to believe that we've come all this way together!"

"Getting back to those interest rates, could you be
a little more specific than 'It's going to cost a pretty penny'?"

"Could I call you back? I'm taking a bath."

"Howard, don't you ever have guilt feelings
about getting ahead of inflation?"

"…and with the power invested in me by Master Charge,
VISA, and American Express, I now pronounce you man and wife."

"You can't repossess it, it's been recalled."

"Nonsense, Brownley. You told me three months ago
you couldn't survive on what I pay you, and here you are...."

"I know that's the correct term, Finley, but couldn't we call them
something else besides 'Sinking Fund Bonds'?"

"Well, that does it for this week's work ethic....
Now for two glorious days of loaf ethic."

"You are charged with getting caught at corporate hanky-panky."

"Okay, which one of you erased Daddy's investment portfolio program
and replaced it with 'Space Invaders'?"

"Actually, we haven't quite decided whether your proposal will fly."

"...but right now the big difference between us is that
I'm drunk with power and you're drunk with Muscatel."

"Marriage is built on trust—the department store
has to trust you, the bank has to trust you...."

"Usury is not a pretty word, Mr. Dunfair."

"My advice is—join the Establishment while it's still there."

"What did you *expect* a financial wizard to look like?"

"And now—a few words about the work ethic."

"If you have to ask the rate of interest, sir, then
perhaps you can't afford the loan."

"I remember when a doubloon was *worth* a doubloon!"

"I admit it was right there on my passbook: 'Substantial
penalty will be imposed for early withdrawal.'"

"If there's one thing money can't buy, Gordon, I've yet to find it."

"Hi! Remember me? As a boy I used to spend hours running my toy cars around your roots. I'm all grown up now and president of a large multinational corporation."

"Just as I thought. We're spending 60 percent of our income
on essentials, and another 60 percent on nonessentials."

"I don't know if this is constitutional or not, but we are
going to say a little prayer."

"If not completely satisfied, return the unused portion of our product
and we will return the unused portion of your money."

"We're a growth company, you know."

"I have the necessities—food, clothing, and tax shelter."

"It says that if you don't order at least $10 worth of merchandise,
they'll give our name to every catalog house in the country."

"I don't know if the working wife is better off,
but her husband sure is."

"Harold doesn't think there should be a Labor Day
if there isn't an Investor's Day."

"First, on the good side, you signed your form
and spelled your name correctly."

"After we take from the rich, why can't we skim a little
off the top before we give to the poor?"